SPIRITUAL ADVENTURES

OF

A PART-TIME YOGI

SPIRITUAL ADVENTURES OF A PART-TIME YOGI

By Dmitri Boulakovski

Editor: Ghada Chadarevian

Published in 2013

ISBN 978-2-9700905-0-2
Swiss ISBN Agency
isbn@sbvv.ch

www.part-timeyogi.com
dboulakovski@gmail.com

Dedicated to my beloved wife, my editor and my inspiration, and to our daughters, who give meaning to our life.

ACKNOWLEGEMENTS

To Catherine Ganson, my English language editor, whose contribution to this book goes far beyond mere linguistic revision, with sincere gratitude for her patience and professionalism,

To Willem Meter, my friend and IT magician, creator of my website, without whom my work would have remained unknown to the Internet reader,

To Andrew Brookes for his valuable help and advice.

Who Am I?

As so many before me, I have often pondered the question "Who am I?" To me this was an existential issue rather than a philosophical matter.

The answer came from a spiritual teacher I once conversed with over the phone. He asked me, "What do you see around you in your room?"

"I see my bookshelves, my posters, the walls, the ceiling, my computer."

"Splendid!" he remarked. "And now, close your eyes and tell me what you see."

"Darkness," I replied.

"Excellent!" His voice was almost ecstatic. "What is it that has not changed?"

"I guess something that perceives both the room and the darkness," I uttered somewhat hesitantly.

"Exactly! Awareness!" He exclaimed. "Awareness! That is what has not changed and therefore awareness is the real you!"

During a workshop that I attended at the Monroe Institute in Virginia to explore various states of consciousness, I experienced, in a state of deep meditation, a complete dissolution of my body into a luminous light.

Although all form vanished, I still retained the capacity to perceive luminosity, radiance and bliss. I became pure consciousness, a minute spot of intense and overwhelming awareness of infinite joy and fulfillment. "This is who I really am," descended on me at that moment, "a spark of consciousness that knows no birth, no death, that may dwell in an earthly body, able to explore physical dimensions, or may exist intangibly beyond space and time."

This led me to the next question, "What has brought this spark of consciousness here, on planet Earth; and why?"

As I look back, I realize that, throughout my life, this question has been, consciously or unconsciously, the force that drives my spiritual quest.

Sri Aurobindo In My Life

I read my first book about Sri Aurobindo at the age of 16, during that endless cold winter, when I spent long evenings alone in my bedroom. It was my brother's first year at university. He lived on campus, away from home. For the first time in my life I had our room to myself, but I was not happy. Loneliness had a bitter taste, and it had to be washed away somehow, by something. That something turned out to be the piano.

I turned once again to the piano, which I had abandoned long ago, after years of diligent practice. At that time - when I decided to give up on my music school - football had become my passion, my inspiration and my fulfillment. I spent entire days on the pitch, training, playing matches or just kicking the ball around with friends. I barely did any homework.

Football took over my life, in fact became my life, the reference point for my relationships, friendships and plans for the future. I started to consider a professional career.

It was at that point that my mother - an opera singer by training who had the angelic patience needed to teach me the art of playing the piano - put it to me in exasperation: "You barely ever come near the piano these days. You have to make up your mind, once and for all. Which is it going to be, the piano or football?"

After all the effort that had gone into my piano lessons, she was sure I would opt for the piano; but it was bad timing. In a couple of days, I was to take part in the most important match of the season. After a short pause, and a long sigh, I expressed my preference for the art of the feet and not the hands. That came as a big shock for my Mom. She practically stopped talking to me. She felt betrayed, and I felt bad. It took months for the awkwardness between us to pass. I still played the piano every now and then, but it was more to please her than anything.

Now, a few years later, things had changed. My footballing obsession had faded into the background. I had changed schools from one of the very worst in town to one of the very best, courtesy of my Mom. She had been dismayed by my intellectual decadence and turned to a friend of hers, a school principal, to extricate me from the unsophisticated environment of our neighborhood.

In my new school, I had a lot of catching up to do. I studied day and night. I abandoned football, old habits and old friends. My brother was no longer home, my parents were at work and, my homework done, I needed to fill my life with something else. I took to reading.

With the same passion I used to have for football, I now started devouring all the books I could lay my hands on in our home library.

Kuprin was my favorite. I admired his unassuming style. He was a fount of knowledge to a boy who was curious about everything. Then I went on to Turgenev, Chekhov and Tolstoy. In just a few months, my perspective on life underwent a Big Bang type of explosion. My head was filled with the lives of people past and present. I changed, I matured, I lived their passions and sorrows, I sank into the depths of their despair and soared on wings of happiness with them. Each chapter took me one step further beyond my boundaries.

It was then that I rediscovered the piano. I was eager to embrace all these new worlds opening up before me, and I needed an outlet to express these new sensations. The magic of music, my friend and confidant, helped me to do just that.

I would put my book aside, savoring for a minute or two the part I had just read, then touch the keyboard, play just one note or a chord, sharing with the silence of the room the mood the book had brought on: my sadness, my joy or my anguish. I would let the sound float out, softly bounce off the walls and drift slowly into the early darkness of a winter day beyond the window, then fade into the incessant cascade of snowflakes falling and covering the ground.

It was then, while looking for the next novel by Tolstoy, that I stumbled on a book on Sri Aurobindo. The photograph on the cover caught my eye. It pictured a bearded middle-aged man with fine features, looking up in calm concentration. I could not take my eyes off his gaze, luminous and unperturbed at the same time. He radiated some unknown power, a boundless power of tranquility. The title of the book was "The Adventure of Consciousness" and its author had a strange name, Satprem.

This was a very different read from Tolstoy. It was modern and challenging. It took you firmly by the hand and led you to the realms of eternal spiritual truth, far beyond our human life and mind. It beckoned you on to infinite bliss and fulfillment, showing all worldly pleasures to be but a bleak shadow of spiritual reality. Once fascinated by the Ultimate, you could never be content with the mundane.

I had found a book that was to change my life.

It described the life and yoga of Sri Aurobindo, an outstanding Indian revolutionary and spiritual master, and his collaborator, the Mother.

Sri Aurobindo was educated in England but came back to India and became a key figure in the struggle to free India from colonial rule. He was the philosophical and ideological father of India's independence. Imprisoned for his revolutionary activities, he spent almost a year in solitary confinement where he had profound spiritual experiences.

When Sri Aurobindo received assurance from the higher consciousness that India would indeed achieve independence, he abandoned his revolutionary work and devoted himself to yoga. Having comprehensively studied various spiritual practices, he went on to develop his own Integral Yoga.

Sri Aurobindo's concept of existence seemed to me simple and convincing. The fundamental reality is Sat Chit Ananda (Sat meaning Existence; Chit, Awareness; and Ananda, Bliss) or Aware Blissful Existence. Out of sheer joy, Sat Chit Ananda creates multiplicity out of oneness.

I see it as the birth of a child. When the baby comes out of the mother's womb, one person, mother/child, becomes two: a mother and a child. In the same way, Sat Chit Ananda produces out of itself infinite worlds and beings in a perpetual "Big Bang".

According to Sri Aurobindo, human beings go through their daily life using their "temporary" personality, a combination of physical, emotional and mental aspects. The "true" personality - the Psychic Being, a tiny spot of consciousness - is located in a subtle body in the area of the heart. Finding the Psychic Being, the true Self, and opening up to a higher consciousness are the two main goals of Integral Yoga.

The road of my spiritual quest was thus mapped out: to discover my true soul, the Psychic Being, and give it control over my life, replacing my temporary personality, a combination of unruly thoughts, emotions and physical impulses; to find a miraculous connection to a vast ocean of supreme consciousness in order to experience it instead of just dreaming about it; and to bring this consciousness into my system to practise the "yoga of the cells".

It would also help if I could develop an inner vision, or clairvoyance, to be able to perceive the subtle reality.

Any one of these tasks would have been a tall order even for advanced yogis who devote their entire lives to self-perfection. What then could I realistically expect to achieve, I, with all my professional and personal plans and ambitions still to be realized? I hadn't a clue how to start. I could only dream. But as someone once said , "The best thing you can do is follow your dreams."

DAVID

In February 1999, I went to India to work at an international conference in the city of Lucknow. I had read in a guidebook that an outstanding guru, Papaji, had lived there. Over the years, thousands of spiritual seekers had come to his talks and meditations from all over the world. He had passed away in 1997, leaving behind a community of followers. I was curious to see the place.

As soon as I had some free time I set out from my hotel, called a rickshaw and went straight to Papaji's house without the slightest idea as to what to expect.

The door was open. I stepped inside and saw a man lying in a deckchair, very relaxed, with his hands behind his head.

"Is this Papaji's house?" I inquired.

"That is precisely what it is," the man said with a humorous smile.

"I just wanted to visit," I said hesitantly.

"Well, you have come at the right moment. We are just about to have dinner. If you pitch in 250 rupees you can dine with the community."

"Sounds great," I said, reaching for my wallet.

"Are you eating with us?" I heard a woman's voice behind me.

I turned around and saw a tiny American lady with kind blue eyes, dressed in a long green Indian sari. She had a voluminous orange turban on her head that made her look both outlandish and touching at the same time.

"If you don't mind," I replied.

"It's good to see new faces," she said. "I'm Baba."

"I am Dima," I said, feeling that Dmitri would sound a bit too official under the circumstances.

About 20 people were sitting around a long wooden table, there was quiet, gentle conversation, punctuated every now and then by bursts of cheerful laughter. When we came up, the conversation stopped and I felt a wave of welcoming curiosity enveloping me.

I saw a bunch of people I had never come across before: casually dressed and easy-going men and women with kind penetrating eyes. "These must be the hippies who have made India their home," I thought to myself.

"Please meet Dima," said Baba.

"Hi, Dima! Welcome! Enjoy your meal," I heard from around the table.

Sitting next to Baba, I told her of my deep interest in the philosophy and yoga of Sri Aurobindo, especially the yoga of the cells, where you invite higher consciousness to descend into your body and transform your physical nature at the cellular level. My problem was, I said, that I did not feel the presence of any higher consciousness and hence this yoga was forever beyond my reach.

"For ever?" she asked. "Who knows? If you come here tomorrow at lunchtime you may meet somebody you can talk to about it."

At noon the next day, I was at Papaji's house beaming with curiosity. Baba was waiting for me at the entrance. Again, she was wearing a sari, a dark blue one this time, unconventionally matched with a bright yellow turban perched on her head. For a few seconds, she looked deep into my eyes and asked, "Are you ready?"

Not quite sure how to react, I nodded with a slight hesitation and smiled. She smiled back and said: "He's here. Lunch has already started." I followed her to the cafeteria. She then pointed to a free spot next to a man wearing a washed-out white t-shirt. I sat down and looked around.

"What brings you to India?" asked the man.

"Business," I replied. "But I could not let this occasion pass without visiting Papaji's house. I have read a good deal about him".

"Hmm… Very good. I also heard from Baba about your interest in cellular yoga," remarked the man, turning towards me. "My name is David."

I looked at him and our eyes met.

He looked right inside me, into my very depths, through my eyes, through my being, into my soul. Our souls met and connected. I could not move or speak. It lasted a few endless seconds. He then closed his eyes with a smile and gently turned away.

It took me a little while to get back to my senses. For a minute or so, I sat motionless, staring at my plate, as if in a daze.

I thought everyone would be watching me, but when I looked up, I realized that nobody was paying any attention. I guessed that spacing out for a few minutes was nothing out of the ordinary here.

After lunch, David invited Baba and me to have a cup of tea at his place. I happily accepted.

We walked from Papaji's house a couple of blocks down the road to the apartment David was renting for the two weeks he was spending in Lucknow. It was a spacious, somewhat chaotically furnished place. We went into the living room with just a few wooden armchairs around a small marble table. David offered me one of the chairs. He sat in front of me and Baba sat on my right.

"There is some tension in the air," David said.

"There sure is!" remarked Baba with a mysterious smile.

David turned to me and looked intensely into my eyes. That had a powerful hypnotizing effect on me. I stared back into his eyes, unable to move. Then, to my surprise, my head started slowly spinning. It moved faster and faster. My whole body started spinning, gathering speed. I had to hold on to the armrests so as not to fall off. My head was filling with golden light.

I closed my eyes, my inner vision seeing spirals of bright energy circling up through my head. This went on for 10 or 15 minutes, perhaps half an hour. Time was no more…

I vaguely felt David get up, go behind me and touch the top of my head. That had the effect of turning the white and golden spirals into one powerful current of light rushing upwards with such intensity that even with my eyes closed it made me blink.

It was frightening. And it was bliss.

The sensation got too much to bear and I exploded into a medley of tears and laughter. One thought was throbbing through my overwhelmed brain: "Can all this ecstasy be just for me? Me alone? It is not fair! Everyone should have it! Everyone!"

Gradually, the room around me was coming back into focus: the ceiling, the windows, the large blue flowers in the vase. I saw David and Baba's eyes – so kind and so happy for me.

"Thank you," I whispered and then added: "Everyone should have it!"

David and Baba only laughed.

They got up and David said, "We will leave you for a few minutes. Enjoy it!"

As David went past, I grabbed his hand and kissed it.

I sat alone in the room with my eyes closed. A current of whitish, golden light was rising through my head. I wanted it to last forever. Finally, I forced myself to get up. Passing by the mirror, I looked at myself. It was the same old me, but with one great difference. In my eyes, I saw an impersonal infinity rushing upwards through my head.

***

I found David alone outside the house, in a small courtyard, gazing at a flock of colorful birds chattering and singing away in a bush in front of him. Looking at him, I felt a surge of intense absolute love and gratitude, such as can only be felt by a disciple for his spiritual master, one who has graced him with the most precious gift of a thousand lifetimes.

He turned to me and smiled.

"Can I hug you?" I asked.

"Go ahead," he replied, opening his arms to me.

It was a memorable, spiritual hug.

Two soul brothers, who had perhaps shared lives upon lives in monasteries, ashrams and spiritual communities in India or Tibet, in Russia or Italy, in Atlantis or Lemuria, who had struggled through the trials and disappointments of the search for the ultimate truth, found each other in an embrace in the city of Lucknow on February 4th, 1999.

"How did you do it?" I asked David.

"Do you know Mother Meera?" he asked in reply.

"No!"

"She is a silent guru from South India who now lives in Germany. She bestows her grace through Darshan."

"Darshan?"

"Yes. By looking into people's eyes she helps them grow spiritually and solve their problems. She knows you, apparently. Maybe not from this life, maybe from a thousand lives ago, and maybe not from this planet, but I had a clear vision that she was ready to connect with you. So all I did was provide a service. I connected you to her light, Paramatman Light."

"What light?" I asked.

David laughed again and said, "Do you know the story about a yogi who lived on an island on the Ganges?"

"No."

"Well, one day, a learned man came by boat to pay him a visit. They discussed various things and, at the end, the pundit asked the yogi if he knew the Latin name of the tree he was sitting under. The yogi said he did not. The pundit told him the name of the tree in Latin and departed. On his way back he thought to himself: This yogi after all is not so wise. He is actually quite ignorant about certain things. As he was thinking that, he saw the yogi running after the boat on water, shouting: Esteemed pundit! Please tell me the Latin name of my tree again! I have already forgotten it."

As I was still pretty much spaced out, I didn't immediately get the joke. My hesitant smile made David laugh: "Running on water. Get it? OK, no problem. I guess it's all been too much for you today."

We went out of the house. I had so many questions jostling in my brain.

"I am filled with all this light now. Will it all be gone tomorrow?" I asked anxiously.

"Once Mother Meera decides to accept you, it is normally for good," David said confidently.

"And where did all this light come from?"

"Well... sometimes a higher consciousness descends into our world in one form or another and, for its own reasons, makes contact with this or that person. It often happens through a guru or a spiritual master. But it can also be by direct touch. It can then soar back into higher realms without trace, or remain connected to a person for good. That person lives in the light, like a child bathing in the radiance of a mother's love."

"Ah... I see."

David called a rickshaw over and asked him to take me to my hotel.

"This will be the most enjoyable ride of your life," I heard his words as they faded into the deafening craziness of Indian traffic.

"Could I see you again?" I shouted into the noise and fumes around me.

But David had disappeared from view.

A Poem

I settled with the rickshaw and was about to cross the street and enter my hotel.

A large group of some fifty school children passed by in front of me, chattering loudly and cheerfully. A few of them looked at me curiously as if they were wondering: "What is this foreign guy doing in our town?" I waved to them and some of the kids waved back.

In the middle of the group, a boy with shining eyes, aged 10 or 11, looked straight at me and smiled, as if to say, "I know all about you". Our eyes met for just a second or two, but even that was enough to recognize another soul whose individuality dissolved into oneness. The group passed by. The boy turned round and nodded. "I'll be seeing you in some future life, in some unknown world," he seemed to be saying. I nodded back.

I suddenly realized I was very hungry and went to have a bite at the hotel restaurant. A couple of colleagues sitting at the bar came over to join me.

"How's life, Dima? Where have you been the whole afternoon? We've been looking for you." They had both had a few beers and were feeling cheerful. I was just about to tell them of my adventure, but instead, despite myself, I mumbled, "I just went out for a little walk in town."

There was an awkward pause.

"And did you see anything interesting?"

"Not really, nothing much."

"OK, Dima. We'll leave you alone with your mysteries. See you tomorrow."

I went up to my room and sat on the bed. I felt confused.

"What's wrong with me?" I asked myself. "Why couldn't I tell them anything? Will I ever be able to share this with anyone?"

I closed my eyes and relaxed into the innocent wordless joy of the carefree light streaming through my head. I opened my eyes and found myself again face to face with my question. It was a question with no answer. I grabbed a notepad and a pen from my bed-side table and started writing.

A Ray of Light

In the grim aloneness in his cell,
He spent his deadly days.
The biting floors, the icy walls,
Had chilled him to the bone.
A ray of light just now and then,
Would penetrate the grey,
When it would lift the stuffy air,
And lighten his despair.

One night he felt,
He could not bear,
The darkness any more.
With all his might,
With all his soul,
He cried out for the ray,
To shed its light not in the day,
But in the thick of night,
At least just once,
For one short breath,
But now, without delay.

That very moment, light arose,
Inside his desperate mind.
He shut his eyes,

His head fell back,
His arms and legs grew numb.

The light grew strong,
The light grew bright,
With a life of its own.
It swiftly rose above his head,
And made him feel aflame.

His soul flew up,
And he was Light,
Not any more just flesh.
He poised, a liberated sigh,
In the waves of deathless skies.

The light went up and round, and round,
Towards the bliss of gods.
His laughter poured down like rain,
In tears of pure delight.

The morning came,
In the dread cell,
The steps of the guard rang out.
He brought a meager meal with him,
For the dweller of the dark.

The guard put down the bowl of food,
And almost turned to go.
But something made him stop...
He sought to pierce the prison's dark.

Hey, help! - He yelled.
They heard his cry,
All guards came to his aid.
There they all stood, spellbound and numb,
And stared at the empty cell.

Handcuffs and chains were all still there,
But not the grey-haired man.
A ray of light lay on his bed...
It seemed as if it laughed.

Mother Meera

February 1999 had been the culminating point of my spiritual life. God-given grace had sent David on my path to open me up to the unending abundant flow of Paramatman Light, a beautiful, caressing energy streaming through every cell and every particle of my being.

Before disappearing behind the fumes of the Indian traffic, David had given me the telephone number of the mysterious Mother Meera, an Indian Spiritual Master, now living in Germany. I had to see her, this person in whose light I was bathing. With bated breath, I dialed the number of her house from my hotel in New Delhi. An Indian man with a pleasant voice answered:

"This is Mother Meera's house, how can I help you?"

My throat constricted and no sound came out.

"Can I help you?" I heard him ask with a touch of impatience.

"Is it possible to see Mother Meera?" I asked, feeling as if this were a laughably impossible request.

"You have to book three months in advance," was his disheartening reply.

"But I need to see her right now," I said, in a way that made the man laugh.

"Really? Is it your first time?" he asked.

"Yes, it is," I replied, regaining a bit of hope.

"Well, you can come then but only for one day," conceded the man.

"I would be happy to come even for one minute!" I exclaimed.

"Really?" he laughed again. "Are you sure?"

"Absolutely!"

"In that case you can come for four days. You will attend Mother Meera's Darshan every evening from Friday to Monday."

"Thank you!! Thank you so much!!" I was ecstatic.

"You are welcome. See you on Friday," I heard his voice in the receiver, still unable to believe my good fortune.

During the whole flight from Chennai to Frankfurt I was on a cloud, in fact I was on top of the clouds, in every sense of the word.

I would fall asleep, only to find myself flying in my dream over a lavish expanse of green valleys and forests in an ecstasy of speed and weightlessness.

"Mother, show me that you are aware of my existence," I would ask Mother Meera in my half-dream. This appeal would often be followed by a rush upwards, towards a bright light, but at that point my consciousness would be eclipsed and I would plunge into the darkness of sleep. After a few attempts, I gave up and just let myself enjoy the light streaming through my head, half dozing, half watching the film that was showing on the plane.

At the airport in Frankfurt, I asked for directions to Balduinstein, the village where Mother Meera lived. I hopped on the train and, in less than an hour, had arrived at my guesthouse, within walking distance of the Magic Place.

Everyone at the guesthouse had come to see Mother Meera, so it was easy to find people to talk to. I learned that Mother Meera had been giving Darshan – the passing of Divine Grace through eye contact – for several years in this tiny village.

She had grown up in India where her uncle had recognized in her an incarnation of the Divine Mother and had devotedly cared for her ever since.

They always travelled together. In Germany, he fell ill and eventually passed away, which was a devastating blow to Mother Meera. She decided to stay in Germany – "in the heart of the wound" as she put it, having in mind the Second World War – and to give Darshan to all those wanting to receive it. Attendance was free; those wishing to contribute could make donations.

The Darshan was starting at seven in the evening. At six, we left the guesthouse in order to get seats as close as possible to the Mother. A tall blue-eyed man at the door checked our names on his list and let us through. The room was full.

I took one of the last empty chairs and looked around. Everyone in the room was very quiet and concentrated, preparing for the appearance of the Mother. I too closed my eyes and tried to collect myself.

All of a sudden, everyone stood up and then once more – silence. At first I did not see the Mother, hidden by the people standing in front of me. I only saw her later, sitting down in a large armchair, facing the room.

After everyone had regained their seats, the silence became absolute.

The Mother sat for a minute in deep meditation, then opened her eyes and nodded. Someone approached and kneeled in front of her. It was her assistant. The Mother laid her hands on his head and remained motionless for some fifteen seconds. She then lifted her hands and the man, still on his knees, looked into the Mother's eyes. Eye contact was maintained for some ten seconds. Then she closed her eyes. The man stood up, bowed to the Mother and withdrew.

The Darshan was to be repeated for the two hundred or so persons gathered in the room and standing outside.

After about fifteen minutes, I gathered up my courage and took my place in the queue to receive the Darshan. Some twenty minutes later, it was my turn. In a daze, I approached the Mother and knelt before her. I felt the light touch of her hands on my head. I was nervous and had no idea what to expect. She lifted her hands… I looked into her eyes…

Her eyes were windows into the infinity of light and power. They were stronger than I was. They were stronger than anyone or anything in the world, and yet that gaze, seeing through my whole being and right into my soul, was gentle and kind.

Her whole self was not of this world. She was exuding love, goodness and compassion, in a way that was almost too much to bear, even for her. I tried to open myself up, my soul, my everything to her gaze, to receive as much light as I could…

She closed her eyes. I bowed, got up and, with some effort, made my way back to my seat.

I stayed quite still for a while, with my eyes closed. I didn't feel very much at first, just a pleasant emptiness. Then came a feeling as if dawn was breaking inside me: a timid whitish light filling first my head and then the rest of my body. This light slowly and gradually grew in intensity, accompanied by a gentle rocking movement deep inside me.

It reminded me vividly of a sensation from my early childhood, sitting on a swing, eyes closed, head back, abandoning myself to the joy of flying – back and forth, up and down – until I no longer knew where I was or who I was or what I should do once the blissful swinging came to an end…

The light and vibrations continued to go their own way without much regard to my capacities. Gentle pleasure turned to intense rapture, which in turn became ecstatic blinding paralysis.

An overpowering lightning jolt of exhilarating energy thundered through the whole of my body, leaving me virtually unconscious and all around me seemed far away and irrelevant.

I was reliving the experience I had had with David in India, there was no longer any doubt as to the source I was connected to: Mother Meera… How was all this possible? It was all beyond my wildest dreams.

Again, as in India, time faded away. There was only Light, nothing else, Light with its intricate movements, its childlike playfulness and its wordless clarity…

Suddenly, I could hear people in the room getting up. It seemed that the session was over. Holding on to the back of the chair, I got up with difficulty. But as people started leaving, I collapsed back on my chair, still shaking from the overwhelming experience.

There was dryness in my mouth and a debilitating weakness throughout my body. Luckily, a few people remained in the room, still meditating, so I did not feel too alone as I came very slowly back to my senses.

The last person left. I got up to go too. I made my way to the bathroom and washed my face in ice-cold water. It helped.

On my way out of the building, I saw one of Mother Meera's assistants at the entrance, watching me with concern.

"Are you all right?" she asked, sounding worried.

"I'm fine," I mumbled very quietly. "I'm very, very fine!"

Yoga of the Cells

After my opening to Paramatman Light, outwardly my life had hardly changed. But in my inner world, the difference was tangible. Whereas before, turning inward would only push me into a morass of mental chatter and chaotic emotions, now, simply by closing my eyes, I could bathe in the soothing, ascending current of blissful energy.

The connection to the Light also helped me to practice the Yoga of the cells, an important part of Integral Yoga.

As I understand it, cellular Yoga is all about reminding cells that they are eternal, and thus, infinite physical life is possible.

Each cell has a mind of its own, resembling that of an infant – innocent, open and life asserting. At the same time, in its subconscious, this mind keeps a memory of the suffering, decay and deaths of many, many lifetimes.

Undoing these painful memories and instilling a firm faith in the infinity of all life in the mind of the cells is the goal of this Yoga.

Holding a dialogue with a few trillion cells is no easy task. It is facilitated by mantras - special words or phrases that have a spiritual meaning. Sri Aurobindo's collaborator in his Yoga, the Sweet Mother, used a well known mantra, "Om Namo Bhagavate", which could be translated as "Oh, the Supreme, I surrender to you, transform me in your image!"

This mantra has been a great help to me in making contact with the cellular level of consciousness. I have also come up with my own uncomplicated invocations.

In my meditations, I try to maintain an image of my cells overflowing with the Light until I have a tangible sensation of rhythmic energy pulsating through my body. Then I start to behave like a choirmaster, mentally addressing my mantra to all the trillions of cells. At some point, I begin to perceive the response of many sweet little voices, happily chanting the affirmations of infinite physical existence. Finally, if the meditation goes well, I simply relax and listen to the hymn of eternal life, sung by my cells, my little friends, without any involvement of my conscious mind.

This meditation is soothing and uplifting at the same time.

Our bodies, our cells, are saturated with consciousness, eager to make a jump to the infinite, aware and blissful existence on Earth. All they need is the initial push and support on the part of our intellect. The mantra of transformation, repeated thousands of times can become a permanent background invocation, penetrating the depths of our subconsciousness.

I will do this yoga till my last breath, hoping that that last breath will never come.

Kerrie

In my quest for spiritual realms, a crucial capacity was missing: inner vision or clairvoyance. I was able to sense energies but I had no inner sight. I realized full well that this faculty was not easy to acquire. Who could I turn to for help? Logically it had to be a clairvoyant willing to share their gift with others. I decided to do an Internet search and the first website I visited was also the last.

I saw a photo of Kerrie, a well-known American clairvoyant. I have seen many pictures of spiritual teachers and found that they often look away from you, as if hiding their eyes from uninitiated observers. Kerrie, however, was looking straight into my eyes from her website picture.

On her webpage, she wrote that we are all angels having a human experience. She most certainly was one. Her all-seeing eyes radiated inspiration, depth and strength. She emanated purity, wisdom and the sort of natural confidence that could only come from the realms of angels, where the essential goodness of all beings is fully revealed.

I decided to call her and ask for an appointment. Luckily, her secretary found a window in Kerrie's busy schedule for a telephone session in two weeks' time.

That period of waiting was in fact good for me as I had far too many questions whirling in my mind. Would she be able to unlock my inner vision? Could she establish contact with my deceased father? Would she assist me in fulfilling my dream to become a writer? It suddenly occurred to me that I was expecting her to solve all my life problems in a single phone session.

"Calm down," I told myself. "One step at a time!"

At last the day of the appointment arrived. Rather nervously, I dialed the number that the secretary had given me and heard a welcoming voice from another continent, "This is Kerrie. What can I do for you?"

I felt at a loss – where to start?

"How are you?" I asked, feeling rather silly.

"I am very fine," the answer came from another world.

I had to start with something.

"My father passed away recently and I miss him a lot. Do you think you can connect me with his soul?"

"Let me see. What was his name?"

I told her.

After a minute or so I heard her voice again.

"Interesting," she said. "He is fine. He chose to be a bird in the subtle world. He is a beautiful golden bird now. He is flying freely from one level of consciousness to another, enjoying his lightness and liberty."

"Does he ever think about me?"

"He does. He is generously pouring the golden light of the Sun of his world onto you, his son of this world. Do you feel it?"

Suddenly, I did. I felt an opening above and to the right of me. I could actually feel the pulsation of a strong and kind energy coming down towards me. A huge smile split my face, a smile of relief and contentment. My father was happy on the other side! I had managed to contact him! That was quick!

"Thank you so much, Kerrie!" I almost shouted down the phone.

"I am glad you can feel him now. I guess you loved him a lot?"

"I did, I do."

"What else can I do for you?"

"Could you help me open my inner vision?"

"Your inner vision? Your third eye?"

"Yes."

"Let me see."

This time the pause was longer.

"It will take a few sessions and some work," she finally replied.

"What kind of work?"

"A bit of rewiring here and there."

"Rewiring?!"

"Oh, don't worry. It's just my terminology," she laughed. "Are you ready?"

"Of course I am!"

A few seconds later, I felt a soothing white cloud entering my head and filling the rest of me. My thinking slowed down and my whole body relaxed and wound down. I was in a light and pleasant daze, in a state of weightlessness, where space and time began to fade away.

I could hear Kerrie's voice as if it were far away. She was describing what she was doing. Frankly, it was all beyond me. This process of "rewiring" was a closed book to me. I started seeing visions of far off planets and inter-galactic spaceships. I was flying through a dark cosmos filled with shining beings of light. They were friendly and unimposing and communicated with me in a wordless but perfectly understandable language.

"I think it's enough for today," I heard Kerrie's voice, slowly bringing me back to my senses.

"I really appreciate it," was all that I could say.

After four sessions with Kerrie all I needed to do was to close my eyes in order to perceive an endless flow of images – glimpses from other realities. These images would be especially bright at night when I would lie in bed, trying in vain to fall asleep. I had to learn to block this flow mentally in order to get any rest at night.

Celeste

In the summer of 2005 I attended an AUM – an all-American meeting of the followers of Sri Aurobindo. It was a great feeling to be among like-minded people, where you don't have to explain yourself. For once I felt I belonged.

Deep down, I was hoping that by some miracle, in this spiritual atmosphere, my true soul, my Psychic being, would be awakened and start leading me through life as a wise and incorruptible guide.

The Sweet Mother once remarked that it takes 30 years of intensive Yoga to achieve that goal. But I was hopeful anyway.

At a side event, one of the participants, Celeste, presented her book on psychic awakening. She also talked about workshops and individual sessions that she conducted to help people attain that state.

After the event, I approached Celeste and asked for an individual session. She accepted, explaining that it would take about an hour and a half.

That session was to become a major turning point in my spiritual life.

I still vividly remember every detail.
I lay down on a massage table and took a deep breath. Celeste sat on a chair at the head of the table and asked, "Are you ready?"

I nodded with a quiet "Yes" and closed my eyes.

Celeste put her hand under my back, moved it to the right and said, "Do you see any images?"

I saw a body lying in the basement of a house in ruins in the midst of snow-covered fields, frozen by the ruthless Russian winter. I had a glimpse of a tank firing at a house at close range in a battle during the Second World War. I then witnessed the agony and death of a young Russian officer in his early twenties. A closer look at him made me shudder. There was something familiar about him. A deep feeling of helplessness and despair overtook me.

"What do you see?" I heard Celeste's voice

I told her.

She then continued, "He needs your consolation. Give it to him now."

I approached the officer and told him: "No more anguish. Peace be with you".

After a while, I heard his voice saying: "Spasibo." (Thank you in Russian.)

"What can you learn from his experience?" Celeste asked quietly.

"Self-forgiveness," I whispered back. "Death is not the biggest failure of life. It is a part of it."

"Now integrate all his sorrow and all his knowledge, because he is part of you," I heard Celeste's instructions.

She moved her hand under my back, looking for the next spot of tension.

A vivid scene sprang up from my subconscious memory. I saw a young pharaoh on a terrace of his palace in Egypt. In the space of a few seconds the story of his life was unveiled to me through my inner vision.

He was an uncompromising and despotic ruler, obsessed with the idea of building a grandiose city. Thousands of workers perished on its construction sites. Thousands more labored without respite to make his dream come true.

The pharaoh acted through a Council of six, his assistants and advisers. The project was using up all the treasury funds but despite the Council's warnings, the pharaoh insisted on completing the construction.

One day, he was invited to a Council meeting in one of the secret chambers of the palace.

Upon arrival, he found only one adviser, the oldest and the shrewdest. He showed the pharaoh in and swiftly left the room, locking the door behind him. Alarmed, the pharaoh knocked on the door, but - no reply...

He tried shouting and threatening to no avail.

A few days later, he lay dying of starvation and suffocation in the wretched chamber, cursing the traitors and imagining the hollow sadness of their faces before the crowd staring at his lifeless body.

"What do you see?" I heard Celeste's voice.

I could not reply. I felt overwhelmed by powerless anger and a burning feeling of hurt, injustice and despair.

When I could finally tell Celeste what I saw, she asked again, "And what is the lesson to be learnt?"

After a pause I uttered, "We should never abuse people who depend on us."

"And now integrate all this pain into the depths of your being, because it is part of your Self".

The search for significant past lives continued. Celeste's palm stopped under my left shoulder blade and I was immediately catapulted into a different reality:

48

I saw a tall man with a shaved head wearing a long white gown. Two assistants were standing to his left, and to his right stood a man with deep blue eyes and a black beard. He was his collaborator, almost his equal. They were inside a large transparent cupola on the ocean's bed – the secret abode of Atlantean priests.

In front of the tall man was a large crystal, Planet Earth in miniature. The bald man was in charge of the Planet's evolution. For thousands of years, his Civilization kept to the path of the Truth, availing itself of material and supramaterial tools needed for its functioning and growth. But around a century or so ago, things started to go awry.

The Civilization that had lived harmoniously as one became fragmented. With fragmentation came hostility and competition for dominance. Selfishness and expediency, treachery and betrayal became commonplace and the higher ideals of the Civilization were abandoned. The tools of evolution turned into implements of war. Set free from ethical imperatives, the base started to prevail over the good. The Civilization's morality deteriorated beyond repair.

The four priests in the cupola were there to decide on the fate of their Civilization: whether to give it another chance or put an end to its existence by rotating the crystal in such a way that the Earth's poles would be displaced and bring about its destruction.

The two assistants were inclined to wait, but the blue-eyed man had lost hope. The final decision lay with the bald man – the High Priest of Atlantis. He was deep in contemplation of his inner vision: the entire history of his people, as well as its likely future, passed before him. He recalled the days of glory, when creativity, refinement and nobility of spirit were revered above all things. The picture changed and he saw corruption and decay taking over. Looking into the future, he could only see degeneration into a despotic rule of the greedy and ruthless over the people, who, in turn, would be reduced to docile obedience and moral prostitution.

The Priest resolutely laid his hands on the symbol of the Planet...

Images of colossal waves and deafening winds flooded the memory of my subconscious. Entire cities were smashed to pieces, as if made of clay, and devoured by a relentless wall of raging water. The Civilization was destroyed in less than a day. In the depths of the Ocean, I saw the priests open the gates of the cupola and join their people in the subtle realms.

Overwhelmed by this horrendous image I broke into tears, my whole body shaken by waves of sobs. I was unable to gulp them down and felt ashamed of myself. Celeste put her hand on my forehead, trying to comfort me.

"I am sorry," I whispered eventually. "I apologize."

"There is nothing that can be done. One needs to accept," I heard Celeste's voice say.

"Was that me?" I asked her. "The priest and the pharaoh?"

"Not necessarily," she replied after a pause. "Shall we carry on?"

The session continued. I had a series of visions of lives spent in monasteries and ashrams, devoted to spiritual search, to the dissolution of the Ego and the rediscovery of the Self. Those images evoked an exquisite sense of spiritual brotherhood, where yogic rigor and discipline blended with a high-spirited sweetness in relationships and a genuine selfless caring for my brethren.

Celeste's hand moved again and stopped in the middle of my back slightly below the heart. Gradually all my attention was absorbed into one spot which was beginning to take on a life of its own. It began to pulsate.

Expansions and contractions were gaining momentum. I could barely breathe. A few more pulsations and the spot exploded, filling my whole being with an intense blinding white light. I took a deep breath into that spot and then exhaled with profound relief.

I stayed motionless for a while, with a silly, happy smile on my face, enjoying the rhythmic pulsations of waves of light, which gently but powerfully enveloped my whole body.

It felt like a culmination of centuries of searching and hoping.

Liberation and bliss... At last... At last...

Some twenty minutes later I sat up, looked around and, not finding Celeste, headed for the door. I stepped out into the softness of a summer afternoon. Across the courtyard I saw James, one of the participants in the AUM, sitting on a bench with a newspaper on his lap. James was a strange fellow; he always looked down, even when talking to you, as if deliberately avoiding eye contact. But this time, he put his paper aside and looked straight into my eyes.

I then understood why he had never done it before. The incredible, steady intensity of his penetrating stare was hard to bear. But now, strangely, when our eyes met, our faces broke into smiles.

James returned to his newspaper and I went to the conference room to look for Celeste. Washing my hands, I glanced at the mirror. Somebody was looking back at me, through my eyes, with a steady, profound gaze of unbearable intensity.

A Poem From Another Life

Celeste was nowhere to be found. She must have left the AUM venue, as she was staying in a hotel nearby. I went back to the conference room and sat through the last presentation of the day. My attempts to focus on the content were futile. I could hear the words but the meaning eluded me.

Instinctively the center of my perception slipped down from my head into my chest and into the middle of my heart. This new center of my being opened up sending a jolt all through my body, exactly as it had an hour ago at the end of the session with Celeste.

With this new perspective, the presentation began to make sense. I was sensing and synthesizing the meaning, bypassing cerebral analysis, grasping the speaker's intent rather than specific words.

Back in my hotel I could not sleep. The images from the session continued to flood my inner vision. I reached for my journal and wrote a poem, line after line, almost without pause, quieting my over-stimulated mind.

Reminiscences of an Atlantean

The twilight of your days had come,
Your days, oh poor relentless Earth.
The dying Sun has touched your ice,
One final time before the Night.

Where are those souls,
Who were your guests,
So pure and proud,
Young and inspired,
Who'd learnt the truth,
But lost their youth,
Drop after drop,
In vain desires?

One soul at least,
On your last day,
Has come to you,
To wish you peace.

My soul, Oh Earth,
My restless soul,
Recalling all!
With no remorse.

I see myself on ocean's bed,
Inside a large translucent sphere.
Three priests I see there to my left,

Sad and resigned before their fate.
Four more are standing to my right,
I see alarm grow in their gaze.
Their lips are mouthing desperate prayers,
All wait for me to cast the dice...

A great round crystal lies before,
I touch it gently with my palms.
That crystal is the Earth itself,
In smaller form, but yet the same.
I hold the Planet in my hands.

Beloved Earth, for such a time,
I cherished you, defended you,
From vicious lies and selfish gain,
From all deserving your disdain.

But then one day I too fell prey,
To soothing voices of betrayal,
To weakness, fear and despair,
I closed my heart to what was fair.

Thus Emptiness became the Law.
We worshipped vanity and dross,
Our slavery was of our own choice,
Our ignorance of our own making.

I looked once more at the bright gem,
My Earth – offended by the fallen race,
One that chose falsehood and disgrace,
With no regrets...

All hope was lost.

I laid firm hands upon the crystal,
Undaunted by my grim intention
It moved… and then the Earth too moved
Into the abyss of redemption.

Auroville

I am once again in Auroville, ten years after my first visit in 1999. Ten years that saw the birth of my second daughter, raising the little ones with my wife, my kindred soul; living in the Light that I was graced with in India a decade ago; struggling through the crushing routine of everyday chores, suffocating anxieties and my father's demise and the greyness of endless winters.

Auroville, the city of dawn, an outlandish village of sweet weirdoes, refugees from Western materialism in the South Indian jungle, enlightened masters in washed-out t-shirts, high-minded aspiring youth, drinking cappuccinos and chilling out on the terrace of the Solar kitchen – the most enlightened terrace on Planet Earth, bathing in Supramental and other kinds of Light, making your head turn as if you were on an intergalactic spaceship, reaching its escape velocity out of the Milky Way.

This place, which might on the surface appear to be a modern hippie hangout, is nothing less than a joint project between UNESCO and the Indian government.

Founded by the Sweet Mother, Sri Aurobindo's spiritual collaborator in 1968, near Pondicherry in South India, it is an experiment in achieving human unity, a daring attempt by a couple of thousand dreamers from all over the world to live together in kindness and friendship without any form of government, authority or police.

Although it has had a bumpy ride, the project, surprisingly enough, is succeeding in sending out to the world the message that a group of responsible, well-meaning individuals are able to manage their material and spiritual lives without any governing structures, finding solutions through compromise and common sense.

We often expect our old friends not to change after years of separation, to be exactly the same, just waiting for us to come back. But Auroville has changed. Its energies strike me as new and refreshing, blending the dense supramental currents with lighter and finer vibrations brought in by newcomers who pass through the red mud roads of the wonder village.

The construction of the Matrimandir temple – the centerpiece and beating heart of the town – was completed about a year ago, giving it an accomplished, grandiose individuality under its golden roof, absorbed in self-contemplation and impenetrable wisdom.

I still cherish my memories – from ten years ago – of the magic in the Matrimandir meditation chamber, where you lose yourself in the dimmed light of the Mother's presence.

Auroville does not readily open its doors to all and sundry. You have to know how to knock, and have the patience to wait for the answer. For the casual, incurious visitor, Auroville is just a chunk of Indian jungle dotted with a few dozen self-absorbed communities lost in tropical vegetation; but for someone who for years has been cherishing the hope of this encounter, the City of the Dawn will open its precious mysteries.

My first connection is Sami, a healer from Germany. I get an appointment with him for a session of shiatsu massage at the Quiet Healing Centre – a beautiful oasis by the ocean with a peaceful garden and a pond with immaculate lotus flowers marveling at their reflections.

Sami is a pleasant-looking young man with kind, penetrating eyes. He asks me if I have any specific health problems. I tell him that after 25 years of working as a simultaneous interpreter at various conferences around the world, my brain feels like a sore muscle and ask him if he could do me a brain transplant. He laughs and says he will do what he can.

I don't know exactly what it is that he does but my head feels like new. Did he indeed miraculously extract my brain, throw it in the bin and fill my head with lotus flowers or perform some other magic?

By the end of the session I am in a bit of a daze. He later explains that after the shiatsu massage, he does the energy work.

I vaguely sense the swift, powerful movements of his arms on top of my head and around my body, feeling, every now and then, currents of air on my skin.

I leave the Healing Centre, half walking, half floating; a standard condition in Auroville.

A sweet breeze from the sea caresses the elongated leaves of the palm trees.

I can't help but smile at the world around me: the sun, slipping peacefully into the Bay of Bengal, a beautiful dog dozing on the lawn, a tranquil pond with lotus flowers that are just beginning to close like the hands of angels, hiding some precious secrets in their palms.

I get on my scooter and drive out of the gate – back into the madness of honking rickshaws stuffed beyond belief with passengers; fumes; cows with beautiful eyes, fearlessly crossing the road, forcing motorbikes into performing incredible zigzags; crowds of people walking unperturbed on both sides of the road, leaving almost no space between them; humongous unruly trucks in a never-ending near-death experience; decomposing buses; phlegmatic bullock carts; and packs of stray dogs curdling your blood with their barking as you pass.

I turn into a quiet street and seconds later I am back in paradise: the Repos beach. It is a cozy community nestled by the sea, mostly French-speaking, consisting of just a few houses around a coffee shop – the true heart of the Repos – serving light meals and delicious cappuccinos.

Step out of the gate and you find yourself on a lively beach: locals sitting on fishing boats turned upside down, gazing at people passing by; elderly French ladies bravely venturing into unruly waves; families of middle class Indian holidaymakers strolling by the sea; and, here and there, grey-haired fishermen, whose fishing gear has remained unchanged for thousands of years, looking dispassionately at the eternal merry-go-round of life.

I jump into the ocean and let the waves lift me up and take me down like a cradle rocked by a mighty but gentle parent. An elderly French lady, swimming nearby, smiles at me and shouts: "Ça fait du bien!" I nod in reply. Absolutely! It really does do you a lot of good! You can forget all the fatigue, the heat and the crazy traffic. You become a happy drop in a carefree ocean.

There is always something exciting going on in Auroville: a talk by an enlightened pundit on some aspect of Integral Yoga; a lecture on Ayurveda or homeopathic treatment; a course on learning Lomi-Lomi massage; an evening of inspired Sufi chants and dancing; or a concert of exquisite classical music by world famous performers who just happen to be in Auroville.

Here, people mind their own business. They go their own way, riding their bikes, scooters or motorcycles, but ask anyone for directions and they stop and do everything they can to help. After all, we are all brothers and sisters here, learning to live together in a new way.

Here, one feels the embrace of the profound mystery of integral transformation into the next species to come on Earth and at the same time one is bathing in an atmosphere of innocence, the innocence of a child who trusts all and everyone around him, certain of meeting with only goodness and kindness.

I walk into the splendid gardens of Bharat Nivas, one of my favorite places in Auroville, and lie down on a bench, overcome with fatigue after a long sweet sunny day. I see huge white clouds like mysterious creatures passing through the infinite blue of the sky. My eyes close and I see the image of Buddha in a temple in Bangkok, his head resting on his arm, his eyes closing for the last time before stepping out of his body back into eternity. Far off, I hear the simple and charming song of a bird.

A deep sensation floods over me – the sensation of reclining into bliss.

Auroville revisited

It was my fourth visit to Auroville. Each time before it had been Paradise found. This time it was Paradise lost.

I got there on 24 December 2011. My family went to celebrate Christmas in Los Angeles. The time difference between India and LA is 13,5 hours. I wanted to wish my loved ones Merry Christmas before going to sleep. I rented a scooter and went to the nearest village to get a local phone card. It was late, I had not slept much on the plane and I was exhausted.

On my way back a couple of dogs started chasing me. I went faster. In the dark, I didn't see a patch of deep sand on the road. The front wheel buried itself in the sand and a second later I was lying on the road with excruciating pain in my left arm and shoulder, covered in dust, unable to take in what had happened…

I slowly managed to get up only to find my left arm hanging uselessly.

An elderly Indian man stepped out of a nearby house, shaking his head in bewilderment: "How did you do it? Are you all right?"

"I don't know, I just fell," I uttered, shaking from the shock and the pain.

The man came up to me and lifted up my scooter.

"Where are you staying?" he asked.

"Just around the corner in the Healing Centre."

"I guess you will need a bit of healing now," he said with a chuckle. "Let me help you with your bike."

He accompanied me to my place, pushing my scooter and trying to cheer me up as much as he could.

I thanked the man and went up to my room.

It was almost midnight. What a way to spend Christmas Eve!

Alone in my room, with a fractured shoulder, in my torn clothes, covered in dust, in the middle of a dark Indian night, enlivened only by the yawl of dogs, I filled a bucket to wash my wounds. Water is scarce in this area, so – no shower. Pour the water on your body scoop by scoop and be grateful.

I called my family to wish them a Merry Christmas, trying to sound as cheerful as I could. I did not have the heart to tell them what had happened to me so as not to spoil their festive mood.

I went to bed but could not sleep, every position seeming equally uncomfortable.

I got up and started pacing back and forth, wall to wall, in my room. I was trying to keep calm and understand what it all meant. One thing was clear.

All that I had planned to do was not meant to be.

Going to every possible massage and treatment, riding my scooter around Auroville and meeting friends, enjoying the thousand and one things that this place had to offer. All that had gone out of the window because of a moment of panic and loss of concentration. I would be confined to my room only able to watch in sadness and despair as all these good things would pass me by.

"Why me?" was rattling around in my head, bouncing from one wall of my room to the other and finally, jumping out and through the terrace. The palm trees outside moved slowly, cradled by the warm wind of a southern night, indifferent to my cries.

I stopped in the middle of the room and asked myself: "What is Life trying to tell me?"

The answer was a deafening silence.

I collapsed into an armchair, trying to find the least painful position for my arm, and – the moment I did – I fell asleep, totally exhausted.

The pink morning light caressed me out of my sleep. I stepped out onto the terrace and all my misery vanished. The light-blue waters of the Bay of Bengal shimmering in the timid early morning sun were gently touching a long sandy beach.

Life itself was soothing my pain in its simplicity and wisdom.

I had a sudden urge to describe this magical moment. I stepped back into the room, grabbed a notepad from the desk, and a minute later I was covering page after page with words of gratitude for the joy of contemplating the beauty of Life. Half way through, I stopped and smiled.

The whole universe was shouting in my face the answer to the question I had asked in the middle of the night.

"This was the only way to force you to write! Haven't you been planning to for the last ten years? You would probably have continued to procrastinate for the rest of your life. Yes, your arm is broken, but it is your left arm, mind you! Your right arm is fine, holding the pen and writing away!"

I smiled to myself and nodded to the immaculate white clouds in the sky, the waves shimmering in the sun and to the tall mighty palm trees. They nodded back to me and whispered: "Patience, patience, patience."

The Cyclone

Four days after breaking my arm I had to face another ordeal. It was an ordeal laid on by Mother Nature going wild.

Around 7 o'clock in the evening, after a beautiful summer day, the wind started to pick up. It whipped up the sea and began to shake and bend the palm trees – first playfully and then more and more violently.

Clouds, appearing from nowhere, turned a warm and pleasant evening into a menacing grey darkness. All of a sudden, lightning hit a palm tree just a few feet away from my terrace. A deafening thunderbolt made me shudder violently, sending waves of pain from my fractured shoulder throughout my body.

I rushed back into my room and closed the door behind me, just in time as a cascade of torrential rain flooded the terrace and a gust of wind smashed a chair against the wall. I sat down on my bed, not quite knowing what to do.

The pressure of the wind was such that rainwater started flooding the room through the mosquito nets that served as windows. I felt as if I were in a carwash with the windows down.

It was a novel experience but not one to be enjoyed for very long, and I swiftly retreated to the bathroom, dragging in the armchair and shutting the door after me, preparing for a long siege.

The bathroom window also consisted of just a mosquito net, but as the wind was blowing from the opposite direction, there was far less water coming in. I ventured once more into the room to rescue my raincoat from the elements. I noted with concern that the water level was rising and leaped back into the bathroom – my refuge for the next 24 hours.

With my coat on and the hood pulled up, I sat in the armchair, trying to be a true yogi by meditating in adverse conditions. That was a real challenge. The wind – a hundred miles an hour, as I later found out – was blowing literally through the house. It felt like a fast train rushing through my refuge and through my body, mercilessly and with no end in sight.

My brain was a wasteland when it came to constructive bright ideas. What was I supposed to do? If I tried to leave the house, I would be instantly smashed by the wind against a wall or a palm tree. Wait for help? Everyone else was in the same delightful situation: stranded wherever they happened to be when the hurricane came on and praying for their lives.

I was trying to concentrate on the image of Sri Aurobindo – the one where he is sitting in an armchair on an open terrace in the pouring rain. Not a drop touches him as he is enveloped in a halo of radiant white light, protecting him from the downpour. He is a symbol of calm and concentration, defying the elements.

Sri Aurobindo used to say Samata, which means peace and calm, is the basis of yoga. Without it, one remains a toy in the unruly hands of human nature, its passions, instincts and desires. Wet and cold, I was trying to feel Samata in my shivering body.

A strange feeling came over me. My consciousness drifted inwards, into my heart and gently propelled me into another dimension.

I saw lush green valleys, embellished by the smooth curves of peaceful rivers of translucent light blue waters. I was flying over dreamy forests of gigantic mighty trees from some long forgotten time.

I marveled at delightful meadows, welcoming lakes and purple mountains, set in deep self-contemplation. It was the land of Samata, imbued with tranquility and quiet joy. It was the land of wisdom and transcendence...

Suddenly I heard a loud knock at the door.

I crawled out of my armchair, walked across the room, water up to my ankles, and opened the door. It was Olivier, the administrator of the Healing Centre, soaking wet, despite his all-enveloping raincoat and high boots.

"Are you alive?" he asked with a grin.

"I think so," I coughed in response.

"In that case, a banana will do you good," he announced happily, handing me one, as if it were a medal for hurricane survivors. "By the way, they said on the radio that this will all be over in a couple of hours. If we manage to fix up the kitchen, we may even have some hot food by the end of the day."

"Is everyone all right?" I asked, recalling that there was a family with children in the Centre.

"Nobody was seriously hurt here or in Auroville," he said. "But I heard a few people were killed in Pondy. And half of the Auroville forest is gone."

I stepped out of the house. The wind had subsided but the rain was still heavy. I looked around. The palm tree forest across the road from the Centre was bent to the ground. Hundreds of mighty trees lying helplessly like wounded soldiers on a battlefield. Huge branches were blocking the highway.

For the first time, there was not a soul on this road normally crammed with traffic. The scene looked apocalyptic.

I went back to my room and out onto the terrace. The giant palm tree, struck by lightning, had collapsed a couple of yards away. I could almost touch its trunk if I stretched out my arm.

"Thank you," I whispered to the poor tree. "Thank you for the two yards."

Energy Healing

Injured or not, I decided to make the most of my time in Auroville. I asked Sami to give me an "energy massage" to facilitate my healing. He kindly agreed. I felt his etheric hands moving through my system without actually touching me. The smooth gentle motions around my body removed the energy blocks, relieved tension and pain, activated and balanced my chakras and sent healing energy to the parts that needed it most.

At some point, I felt my awareness dissolving into space around me, leaving me in a pleasant trance. Later on, I found out that, at that moment, Sami had connected with my astral body and cleansed the subtle grid linking the energy body to infinity. I was fascinated by what he did, and asked Sami if he could teach me how to work this miracle. He looked at me with his inner vision – eyes half closed, seeing the image of my subtle bodies.

"You are a healer," he said with conviction. "I can teach you. You should remember that it is your aura that heals. In fact, never try to heal anyone. You should just accompany a person's energy and the healing will happen of its own accord. Simply ask the higher consciousness: what is this person's next step towards Unity? And then follow your intuition. Do you understand?"

"Yeah," I said eagerly, happy to be accepted as a disciple. "All right," said Sami with a smile. "The first lesson will be tomorrow at 11 in the morning at my place."

For once in my life I was half an hour early for an appointment. Sami was finishing his session with a client. I sat on a bench in front of his house gazing at the huge, peaceful, powerful trees surrounding his house. The community he lived in truly merged with the jungle. The air was filled with the strong and potent smell of exotic flowers. The incessant chorus of birds of all shapes and colors had a calming effect on me.

I closed my eyes and allowed my senses to reach out and touch the trees and the leaves with my invisible hands, caress the birds and rest my ephemeral cheek on a far-away cloud drifting through the deep blue sky…

"Are you ready?" asked Sami, abruptly shaking me out of my meditation.

"Yes, I am, absolutely!" I replied, getting up from the bench and rubbing my eyes, trying to get back to the here and now.

"Good. Let's go upstairs and you will show me your abilities!"

As I was following Sami into his room, I was seized by a brief but shattering crisis of self-confidence. "What capacities am I going to show? I don't have any! What am I doing here? I should just drop the whole thing!" But it was too late.

"Imagine you have invisible hands," was Sami's first instruction.

"I already did that just a few minutes ago," I thought to myself with a smile.

"OK," I replied.

"Good. Now put your invisible hand inside my shoulder and move the energy down to my hands."

I kind of imagined it and kind of did it.

"Hey, not so hard! Go slow!"

"Did you feel anything?" I asked in amazement.

"Oh yeah, and very much so! Go gently! Always follow the energy, never push it!"

Not quite understanding the concept of following the energy, I tried anyway.

"Much better! Now you've got it. Now hold your hand on top of my chest and tell me what you feel."

Oh miracle! I did feel a strong pulsating current of energy coming from the middle of Sami's chest.

I guess I looked a bit silly and Sami could not help laughing.

"What do you feel?"

"I feel a current of energy touching my palm," I replied, bewildered.

"Excellent, this is my heart chakra. Now move this energy clockwise with your hand, as if opening and cleaning a vortex of energy."

"OK," I mumbled hesitantly.

The energy current indeed did follow the movement of my hand forming a well-shaped vortex.

"Now put your hand inside the vortex, remove anything that blocks the flow and offer it to the blue light of Mother Mary."

Following Sami's instructions, I did feel some substance interfering with the energy movement. I grabbed it from underneath and pulled it out. It even seemed to burn my fingers.

I pictured a sphere of blue light on top of my head and I channeled the nasty substance away into the blue space. The burning sensation stopped, which probably meant that my mission was accomplished.

"Not bad for a first time," said Sami. "You need to practice now. Work on your own self. Move, clean and harmonize your own energy and chakras. Anyway, all this is happening in your mind, so it doesn't matter whether it is you, or another person in front of you, or someone a thousand miles away. Mind and energy know no distance!"

"And now one more thing," He added. "We always finish the session by cleaning the client's astral body. In your mind, move out of my etheric aura and clean the grid of my astral body."

By then I had stopped asking questions and clarifications. I just tried to do what Sami told me to do. Suddenly I found myself in a marvelous space. I breathed a deep sigh of relief like a swimmer surfacing after a long dive. Everything around me felt light and cheerful, breathing was easy as if in an atmosphere of pure oxygen and the predominant color around me was bright purple.

"How do I clean the grid, and where do I find it?" I inquired quietly from this enchanted world.

"Just feel the subtle lines forming the grid stretching out into infinity. Try to arrange them in perfect order. Then remove from the astral body anger, frustration and any other negativity."

I had only a vague sensation of the grid and could not find much negativity in Sami's astral body. I guessed he was evolved enough to keep his energy system calm and peaceful.

"OK," he said finally. "It is enough for today. Enjoy the rest of your day and I'll see you tomorrow. I don't think you'll have much trouble sleeping tonight. You have worked hard. They say, one hour of energy work is the equivalent of five physical massage sessions, so rest well."

I walked out of Sami's house in a pleasant state of light hypnosis, deeply relaxed and feeling my physical body as if from a distance. On my way out, I had to pass by a field, surrounded by a low fence, where half a dozen cows were grazing peacefully.

Suddenly, a large black cow, probably stung by a bee, started galloping violently around the field, jumped over the fence and charged towards me. It stopped abruptly a couple of steps in front of me, breathing heavily and staring menacingly. Behind me was a stone wall and I had nowhere to go. The shepherd was looking away and unaware of what was happening. My situation was strange and dangerous.

Something inside me whispered: "Talk to the cow's astral body!" I closed my eyes and moved inwards, trying to picture the astral body of the beast. I found myself in a dry yellowish space filled with splashes of red and orange. "Calm down, all is well," I muttered inside my head, trying to turn the red and orange flashes into a cool blue light. "Please calm down and walk away."

I opened my eyes. The cow was still in front of me. But something had changed in its gaze. It was no longer angry and obstinate but rather dull and indifferent. A second later it moved away and strolled back to its grazing ground.

Wasting no time, I swiftly walked out of the gate, my heart pounding in my chest.

A Sufi Evening in Downtown Geneva

I was back in Geneva from India. Back to the sterile comfort of Western life and back to the greyness of the endless winter.

One day, my wife and I were invited to attend an evening of Sufi chants and prayers at a downtown bookshop, known for organizing offbeat cultural events. We readily accepted the invitation as it gave us a chance to discover a fascinating tradition, practically unknown to us.

From the very start, I was struck by the cacophony of energies in the room. We were a strikingly diverse group of some thirty people on our way to an unknown destination.

As soon as the lights went off, an uneasy silence enveloped the room. The newcomers were sitting on one side, and on the other I could vaguely distinguish the outlines of women with their heads veiled, their features barely discernible in the dark. Among the newcomers were two visitors from Saudi Arabia, wearing Gucci headscarves, a young woman on a quest and a blue-eyed man, clearly an old hand at such events, who was having a quiet conversation with a very Western-looking Sheikh.

In the middle of the room, three other Sufi, all of them Arabs, were tuning their instruments, preparing for the ceremony.

A few minutes later, the Sheikh joined them and started the *dhikr* – the Sufi ceremony of invocation and remembrance of God.

With my eyes closed, I felt a certain heaviness, a malaise in the room. I tried to see, with my inner vision, the auras of people around me. Some were shining brightly, others were closed and heavy.

I tried knocking on every door, waiting for an answer, for an opening. Some moments later, doors started to open, one after another, some readily and some more reluctantly. A man sitting next to the Sheikh, Saheed, started chanting. His voice was fresh and sincere. The group was building up a common energy, discordant as yet, but here and there with flashes of unifying light.

I concentrated on my wife's aura. She had recently gone through a traumatic experience. Her much-loved uncle had passed away. Her aura had shrunk and was clinging to her body like a *peau de chagrin*. I tried to open the passage of light on the top of her head. It took a certain amount of effort, but gradually her aura started to expand. She breathed a deep sigh of relief but still looked weak and fragile.

Memories of our first meeting came flooding back. We had met in Yaoundé, in Cameroun at an international conference. I had gone to a restaurant with a group of friends and colleagues where I found myself sitting next to a beautiful young woman, radiating kindness and intelligence.

We introduced ourselves and exchanged a few words, but otherwise the conversation was general. "What a charming and sensitive person," I thought to myself.

The next day, at breakfast, I saw her sitting a couple of tables away from me. We exchanged smiles and suddenly a strange vision came to me.

I saw the two of us sitting together in a restaurant at a round white table in a garden. The scene was a snapshot of our life some twenty years on. I saw her face very clearly: her tender penetrating look, full of love and strength. Her dark hair was embellished by a few silver threads. She was wearing a warm light brown scarf – it was a bit chilly outside. We were having the sort of intimate conversation that could only take place between people who have been together for many years.

The image gradually faded and when I looked at the table where she had sat she was gone.

It was the last day of the conference. I went up to my room and looked out of the window. A group of colleagues were loading their suitcases onto a bus. She was among them.

I rushed downstairs. She had just paid her hotel bill and was heading for the bus. She smiled when she saw me and said, "It was a pleasure to meet you." I couldn't think of anything to say. It was embarrassing. The bus was waiting for her. Suddenly, to my own surprise, I said, "What do you think about a long-term relationship?"

"What?" She looked at me totally bewildered. "We barely know each other. I am really sorry. I have to go now."

"Just think about it," I whispered, desperately watching her as she headed for the bus…

Now, twenty years later, here we were, sitting next to each other in a bookshop in Geneva, holding hands, carried away by the magic of the Sufi chanting.

The build-up of energy in the room reached its peak. The Sheikh stood up and started whirling, passing into a trance, with one arm high above his head pointing upwards and the other extended downwards.

With each turn, he sent out waves of energy towards us. The whirling accelerated and his large body seemed to be carried on a current of wind that only he could feel.

The music stopped. The Sheikh sat down, still in a trance, the whirling motion still continuing within him. My wife, exhausted, bent down, her chest on her lap, remained motionless for a while.

Then, out of nowhere, a miracle occurred. A deep and tangible sensation of love descended into the room, washing away the tension, the prejudice and the malaise, like a sea wave casually bringing down a sandcastle on the beach. A child-like innocence reigned in our hearts.

Everyone in the room was my beloved friend.

The lights came on. My wife and I got up, still holding hands. A young man approached us and offered us dates on a tray. Our eyes met, and there was no "other", just light and kindness, a meeting of kindred souls.

The Gateway Program

I had been dreaming of visiting the Monroe Institute for many years, from the time that I read Robert Monroe's trilogy on his out-of-body experiences.

The Monroe Institute in Virginia is a center for consciousness studies. It was there that the hemispheric synchronization, or Hemi-Sync, technique was discovered. Hundreds of CDs featuring this technique were produced to help people improve various aspects of their lives.

The Institute is also known for its work in mapping consciousness or identifying vibrations corresponding to its various states, including out-of-body experiences.

Deep inside, that is exactly what I wanted: to go beyond my physical body and explore other realities, meet non-physical guides and helpers who could introduce me to magical worlds and dimensions, and finally unite with my higher self, transcending questions and answers, and live in the Truth.

How realistic was all that? I had no idea. But I certainly wanted to find out.

In August 2011, I was visiting New York with my family at the insistence of my daughters, who had grown up in a small Swiss village and at the ripe old age of 11 and 14 had not yet been to the Big Apple. They wanted more than anything to see it and made no bones about it to their parents.

My own desire to spend two whole weeks of my vacation in the city that never sleeps was not quite as strong, and I made a deal with my guys. I was to go to Virginia, to the Monroe Institute, to attend a six-day program called "The Gateway Experience" and spend the rest of the two weeks with them. Fortunately, my adorable wife acquiesced, the girls did not mind and the deal was struck.

A van, sent by the Monroe Institute, picked me up with two other participants at the Charlottesville airport and half and hour later we reached our destination. I went to my room.

My bed, equipped with headphones and speakers, resembled a sound-and-light-proof cabin, a CHECK unit in local jargon. I was to spend many hours in it, headphones on, listening to hemispheric synchronization recordings blended with music, verbal instructions and specific frequencies that would transport me to unknown dimensions.

In the evening, all the participants got together in a small wooden house known as "Bob's cabin". After introducing ourselves, we listened to a briefing about the institute and the program for the week, given by our moderators Penny, Bob Monroe's daughter and John.

The Energy Balloon

The following morning, we started with an exercise called Focus 10: "body asleep, mind awake". Focuses with numbers were names given by Bob Monroe to various states of consciousness.

To get to that state you have to go through a relaxation process, guided by Bob Monroe's quiet clear voice. One can tell right away that Bob used to anchor radio shows.

Along the way you are supposed to imagine a solid box, where you put all your anxieties and concerns so that they don't bother you during your inner journey.

This I did very happily: "Arrivederci all my fears and worries!" I said in my head, thumping down the lid of the imaginary box.

Next came the "resonate tuning" part where you breathe in fresh energy and exhale all your fatigue with a buzzing sound, creating vibrations throughout your body.

That was followed by creating a protective energy balloon around me by imagining light coming out of my head, going round my body and entering the soles of my feet.

And then a strange thing happened:

I was flying over a cemetery – a few dozen gravestones, lit by the afternoon sun against the backdrop of yellowish sunburnt grass. The whole place looked deserted and sad.

Suddenly I heard somebody say: "There is nobody here. They all went to the beach."

Startled I asked: "Where is the beach?"

"Just go downhill and you'll hit it," was the reply.

The next moment, I was hovering over a wide stretch of perfect white sand. I saw people sunbathing, playing volleyball and jumping into ocean waves. I looked up and saw a dozen semi-translucent persons, holding hands and dancing in a circle, around fifty yards above the ocean.

"These must be the people from the cemetery," I thought to myself.

An idea crossed my mind. "It would be good to invite my gateway group here."

In a split second I saw three or four participants joining me. Holding hands, we started circling around joyfully in the sky on top of the ocean waves. Then one of us said, "Let's invite the rest of the group!"

We called out their names and gradually they joined us. Still holding hands, we formed a circle and began, one by one, doing somersaults, laughing like children.

Then somebody cried: "Let's dive!"

We all happily did so, jumping in and out of the water like dolphins.

After each session the group would go to the conference room for debriefing and sharing experiences.

I shared mine and then added: "It was so vivid. Could I really have made it up?"

Penny, a remarkable psychic and just about the kindest person I have ever met, asked me: "And how does it feel afterwards?"

"For almost an hour, kind of ecstatic," I replied quietly.

Penny did not comment. She only smiled and gave me an enigmatic look enveloped in eternal mystery.

Bye Bye Body

"This is Focus 12: "expanded awareness". You will go far beyond the limits of the physical body". I listen to the words of the facilitator and feel the excitement building up inside me. Adventure time! All aboard! The spaceship is departing in three minutes!

I was indeed in for a ride but of a different kind.

I was flying on the back of a huge animal. Powerful rhythmic movements of enormous wings were sending vibrations all over my body. At first I thought I was on the back of a flying dinosaur, some kind of pterodactyl, but then somehow concluded that a flying dinosaur must be a dragon.

The dragon's skin was smooth and cool, getting a bit rough on the bumps I was holding on to. The sensation of flying was exhilarating. I felt powerful and free. Down below I saw lush valleys and gigantic trees. We were flying over a lake and I asked the dragon to land next to it. When it did, I stepped down and the dragon flew up into the whitish blue sky.

At the debriefing I said: "I had a Hollywood experience. I flew on the back of a dragon. I guess I must have watched Avatar too many times. But it sure felt good!"

The Energy Bar

In this new exercise, we were supposed to examine our bodies and discover any ailments. We then had to imagine a bar of light or energy that we could use for healing.

Inspired by my first experience, I almost jumped into my CHECK unit.

The beginning was promising:

There was an image of me riding a beautiful white unicorn, running steadily and powerfully through a forest of enormous trees, dignified and benevolent in their might.

The early morning mist was fading, opening up vistas of fields and valleys to my left. The air was filled with the happy chatter of birds, and in the background, every now and then, I could hear the deep voice of an owl, as if warning me of something…

The next moment, the forest started getting thicker. Making my way through the bushes became harder. It was getting cold too. Snowflakes began to fall on the branches of the trees. Everything around me looked grey and lifeless.

I realized I was entering deeper and deeper into my physical body.

I thought to myself: "Is that how it is then, my body? A stiff dark forest, paralyzed by the cold of a merciless winter?"

Depression and hopelessness began to overwhelm me, as I was unable to bring so much as a spark of life or light into this frozen desert. I felt tears of despair running down my physical cheeks and I was too ashamed to sob, afraid to bother my roommate.

I found it harder and harder to breathe. I felt I was running out of time and didn't know what to do...

As Bob's voice started the countdown to get me out of this nightmarish meditation, a miracle happened:

A powerful movement swept away the dreadful forest. In its place, I saw hundreds of fresh sunflowers, springing up as if by magic, out of the ground and, a second later, I marveled at a huge golden field, extending as far as the eye could see...

Sheer joy extinguished my depression as I rolled out of my bed and rushed out of the room and into the light of day.

Out of time

Focus 15 was introduced to us as a dimension without time, a space of deep stillness and calm.

Well… It happened quite differently for me.

The meditation started, but I could not go inwards at all. My thoughts were still in the conference room with the group. In my mind, I was still savoring some of the little jokes that we had exchanged. I was embraced by a warm feeling of pure love for a wonderful bunch of people brought together by the program: sincere, open-minded and a lot of fun.

In the meantime, Bob's voice was already counting to 15, and I realized that I was in danger of missing out on the entire NO TIME experience. I did not even bother to close my eyes, gazing at the darkness of the CHECK unit. I turned my eyes down, then to the left and…

Saw a spacious room in a large, somewhat dilapidated mansion. Suspended in the air, I could see the inside of the room from a point just below the ceiling. Down across the room, there was a long table. A dozen people were seated around it in silence. In the middle was a man wearing a long white robe. His face looked tired.

I felt his deep, unspoken loneliness as if there was not a soul in the world that he could relate to. He looked up at the last ray of light entering through a small narrow window and said: "One of you will betray me..."

The next sensation is that of agonizing consciousness departing the mutilated body nailed to the wood.

The point of perception is rapidly moving upwards, still facing the scene that is getting smaller and smaller.

There are two men approaching the body. They look tiny in the distance.

The perception slowly turns upwards, away from the Earth, facing more and more the opening skies...

The whole vision lasted a few short minutes but left me in shock.

I sat up in my bed and threw off the headphones.

I was in the dark, sweating and breathing heavily, unable to understand where all this had come from. Was it the influence of the collective subconscious or archetypal dreams?

I still don't have an answer.

To Be or Not To Be: a Matter of Choice?

Focus 21 was the last of the Gateway programs. It corresponds to the last state of consciousness within human existence before dying.

During the introduction of Focus 21 by our facilitators, there was a somewhat anxious silence in our group, as it might be in the dressing room of a team, getting ready for the final game of a World cup.

All sixteen of us were looking inwards, into our very depths, as if asking: "Will I be up to it, will it finally happen, the thing I came here for?"

I knew that some of us had come in the hope of meeting our dear departed: parents, brothers and sisters. And for some, so far… it had not worked. Others were looking for answers: "What to do next in life; can I rebuild a relationship; will I find a job that will not be killing me; will I ever be able to live a life that brings a smile to my face; can a sickness be healed; can a beloved soul be saved or is it too late?"

We are all full of such questions. Would this last trip to the other side of reality bring an answer?

I had come here to meet my higher self and this was my last chance.

For the last time I closed the curtain of my CHECK unit. Headphones on, speaker volume to normal, I reach for the switch to turn the ready light on and… off we go!

Throughout the build-up to Focus 21 my mind was in turmoil: I mumbled the relaxation commands, messed up the tuning and the balloon business and approaching Focus 21, I very simply and primitively passed out into sleep.

"Oh Great!!!" was the last bitter thought that went through my mind…

I came back to my senses from a vivid and rather scary sensation of speed – the speed of flying inside a whitish tube, stunned by its various twists and turns. I was going so fast that I could neither think nor breathe, but only watch the tube end of the white space as it zigzagged in front of me.

This rollercoaster ride lasted a minute or so, and at the end of it I dropped out of the tube and stopped, suspended in what appeared to be a dense bright white liquid.

By moving my body I floated up and felt it dissolving into white light with an exhilarating feeling of liberation. All the pains of the flesh are gone. Gone is the fear of sickness, weakness and suffering. Gone is fear itself... of anything at all!!!

I was an ocean of blissfully pulsating radiance without any shape or form or limits. At last – freedom from the body, freedom from individuality, personality, ego and all that nonsense. Finally, I am who I am: infinite smiling contentment.

A minute passed followed by another. The Bliss is still there. The Light filled with consciousness...

And then this consciousness suddenly asked: "Is this the higher self that you were looking for? If it is, then there is no self to it at all. There is no such thing as an individual higher self. There is only an impersonal existence. One for all. One for all, my dear..."

Out of curiosity I started pushing the point of consciousness, which I had turned into, downwards till I reached a certain level where my body began to re-emerge.

At first it was just a transparent image of me. Semi-translucent and still bathing in the delicious white light. Further down there was a level of solidification, where my body resumed its normal shape, but was still soaked in the blissful nectar. Down a bit more – and here we go – back to human existence.

The sounds in the headphones faded, the facilitator's soft voice called us to the conference room, but I still could not move a finger, still fully embraced by the rhythmic pulsations of the bright white rapture.

Finally, I made it out of my room and, holding on to the rail, with wobbly knees, started going up the stairs.

I was overwhelmed by my discovery: how quickly and easily we dissolve into an impersonal infinity, without a trace of any form or shape. We are indeed passing waves on the face of the ocean, our separateness lasts for a lifetime, a split-second on the clock of eternity, before returning to the vast unity of a vast mass of blissful consciousness.

We are always just a small step away from losing our human form!

Suddenly, all the fascination that our world has for the individual and the personal, appeared to me to be a gross and extravagant exaggeration. To think of all the volumes written on the intricacies of the ego; hundreds of thousands of shrinks trying to figure out their patients' individual problems; millions of people losing their lives in wars for causes that just a few years later lose their meaning; trillions spent on weapons that turn into scrap metal as technology advances and as the worst enemies become the closest allies.

Why don't we simply abandon our individual and nation-state selfishness and live as one humankind: grow together, suffer together and transcend ourselves together?

A spontaneous vision came before me:

Planet Earth was a huge ball filled with a shiny warm light. Everywhere I looked, I could see people: some were emerging from the light and whirling, like Sufi dancers: others were making elongated, slow-motion jumps, poised in the air and then diving into the light and disappearing in the shimmering vastness, only to reappear on the surface seconds later to continue this celebration of oneness.

Strangely enough, that seemed real to me. Much more real than our grey existence, misguided in its illusion of separateness.

When I came to the conference room, the debriefing was almost over. I sat down, still a bit shaky, leaning against the wall.

It was my turn to speak. I related my experience. I said that the Higher Self that I had met belonged to all and that I wished the entire group had been with me in that miraculous place between the form and the formless.

One of the participants said that he had finally met his mother who had left her body just a few months ago. He said that he had given her a big hug. He also saw his father, who was still alive, joining them in this shared expression of family love.

The atmosphere in the conference room was charged with a feeling of connectedness and compassionate understanding. Then we all got up and – holding hands – sang "OM" all together.

I felt waves of pure love passing around in a circle from one heart to another.

Lifeline

One year later I got lucky again. I went to Spain to another Monroe Institute retreat called the Lifeline program. Lifeline is about retrievals. It is about finding souls who have got lost in the labyrinths of non-physical worlds after death and inviting them to the "Park" or the "Welcome Centre" for departed souls.

The place for newly departed souls

At my very first try, I managed to release the pain that had been tormenting me subconsciously for the last fifteen years.

As soon as I found myself in the place of after-death confusion, I saw my mother. I had had no contact with her since she had died fifteen years ago.

She was sitting in a dark cave, high up in the mountains. She looked lost and deeply confused. Years of isolation and despair had paralyzed her will. She spent her days in weary idleness. It was heartbreaking to see her in that condition.

I flew over to the cave and sat right in front of her. Her expression changed instantly. Her look was startled but filled with so much love. "Dima!" She exclaimed. "How did you find me?"

Instead of answering, I said, "Shall we go and find Papa?"

"Do you know where he is?" she asked, a little perplexed.

"Of course I do," I replied, keeping my fingers crossed he would be at the Park.

After my father had passed away two years ago, I contacted a clairvoyant in the US asking her to help me re-establish contact with him. It had taken her just one session to do that. But I had been unable to reconnect with my mother no matter how hard I tried, whether by myself or with the help of others. I had found that bitterly disappointing.

And at long last there she was!

Face to face and holding my mother's hands, I started moving towards the Park. After a short flight upwards, we landed on one of the Park's alleys and walked towards the banks of a large lake.

I turned to my left and saw my father walking swiftly towards us with a big happy smile on his face. On this occasion, he was a young man again, in his mid-twenties, handsome and energetic.

He hugged us both and we stayed still for a minute or so in silence, embraced by Love beyond expression, full of joy at the family reunion.

A few moments later, we realized that we were surrounded by other departed family members. My mother and father turned to them in amazement.

I saw my mother's two cousins who had left their bodies shortly after my mother's death. I remember how at the time I had been struck by the fact that they had left this world in the same year, despite their age difference.

I saw my mother's brother who had passed away in his early forties; something my mother had been unable to come to terms with for over thirty years.

My two grandmothers, whom I had never met as they had died young, were both there, looking incredibly sweet and noble. I also saw close friends of my parents who had been like family to us.

The whole group was united by a harmony of rapture, absolute love, kindness and happiness. These souls had come together and endured the untold sufferings and hardships of the 20th century: war, repression and deprivation.

They had come here to meet the challenge of surviving against all odds and they had survived. That had required great strength, purity, nobility of spirit and detachment from all things material. They had miraculously succeeded and now they were celebrating.

They were celebrating in the same way they did everything else: throwing themselves wholeheartedly into the moment. When they loved, they really loved; when they laughed, they really laughed and when they hugged, you knew you'd been hugged – beyond any doubt. They were chatting away about things that had happened to them on Earth and beyond, over the decades that had passed before this moment.

I stood there watching them with a warm feeling in my heart, but with a growing sensation of being left out. I began to realize that I did not truly belong to that group – I belonged to a different generation. Their mission had been to survive, ours was to grow and develop, with the hope of giving our children the chance of a better life.

Suddenly a huge beautiful white sailboat emerged on the lake and neared the embankment. That did not seem to surprise anybody. Still chatting happily, now totally oblivious of my presence, the whole group – my parents, family and friends – started boarding and as soon as the last person had got on board, it sailed to the middle of the lake then floated up towards the sun and disappeared in an explosion of dazzling light.

I stood on the embankment totally dumbstruck. Not one of them had even bothered to say good-bye! After these fleeting moments of happy reunion they were gone, and probably gone forever! I could not believe it.

I was deeply sad but at the same time I was happy for them. They had all seemed so delighted, almost ecstatic. They had probably been waiting for my Mom, the last missing member of the group. As soon as she had rejoined them, they were free to leave this planet – to click out, as Bob Monroe put it – and move on to other realms, to continue the never-ending adventure of the Soul. Our life on Earth no longer had any relevance to them. They did not co-vibrate with our half-hearted materialistic existence and were counting the days to move on.

Basil

In my next rescue mission, I was to retrieve a part of myself. Shortly after putting my headphones on and adjusting a pillow behind my back in order to sit comfortably, I began to see a wealth of images.

I was flying over a strangely familiar landscape. My attention was caught by a simple white cross in the courtyard of a church. It looked lonely and abandoned.

I circled around it in the air and then landed in front of it. As soon as I did so, the figure of a Russian Orthodox priest rose from the grave. In a flash his whole life was laid bare before me.

His name was Basil. He had been born in 1805 into a priest's family in the city of Mtsensk. His father was a kind-hearted but weak man, finding refuge in religion. His mother was a strong-willed and uncompromising lady, shouldering most of the burden of bringing up Basil and his three sisters.

Basil took after his father. He was a lonely boy, indecisive and inclined to procrastinate, often punished for his forgetfulness and constant daydreaming.

As was customary, his parents sent him to a seminary. He found his religious studies boring and frustrating. One year before graduation, he was sent as an intern to the Saint Basil monastery in Greece. That voyage was a bright spot in the otherwise uneventful period of his studies.

He made friends with a Greek monk called Nicholas who one day took Basil to the sacred cave in the cellars where outsiders were never allowed. He told Basil to keep it a secret. In that cave, the skulls of deceased monks were kept from times immemorial.

"Look!" said Nicholas, pointing to the skulls. "They are all smiling, ready to embrace life in Heaven. Is it not inspiring?"

Basil looked at the skulls and shuddered. Hundreds of monks were looking at him radiating joy and contentment through the eye sockets in the skulls. For them, the long-awaited moment had come, time to leave the flesh and embrace heavenly existence.

Basil stood in silence, unable to move. That moment changed his life. For the rest of his time on Earth, he would patiently await the liberation of his afterlife and spiritual fulfillment.

After graduation, Basil was sent to a church in a small village some fifty miles away from his hometown. His uneventful life and the uninspiring parish turned him into a sad and bitter loner, spending most of his time in the seclusion of his little house on the outskirts of the village, dreaming of post-mortem delights, and often ending his day drinking heavily to chase away the misery of earthly life.

I was still standing in front of the grave but Basil himself had vanished.

Intuitively I went to Focus 23 – the land of stranded souls – and instantly found Basil in his lonely home, at the end of his tether, still waiting for liberation.

It was time for me to act. I tried to fill myself with as much bright light as I could and I entered Basil's abode. He looked at me in surprise and disbelief.

Trying to sound as solemn as I could, I asked him: "Are you ready to embrace the light?"

He looked at me somewhat sardonically and replied with a smile: "I have been ready for the longest time but have not had a chance so far."

Facing each other and holding hands we went up to Focus 27.

I saw Saint Basil himself waiting at the gate. My poor Basil, my own tormented former incarnation, rushed frantically towards the Saint and disappeared in his light.

My mission was accomplished.

Helping Other Group Members

Next we were supposed to seek out any significant incarnations of other members of the Lifeline group. My task was to explore the past lives of my roommate Michael.

I tried to concentrate on his aura before drifting off to other worlds, to the sound of Bob Monroe's voice. The period of darkness went on for rather a long time and I started to feel frustrated.

The darkness suddenly dissipated, as if somebody had lifted a curtain, revealing a vivid scene. I was hovering over a beautiful park in England. A lady was strolling along a broad alley, exchanging brief greetings with others from time to time. She was exquisitely dressed and carried herself with an air of calm dignity.

My invisible helper told me that this was 1781, that the lady's name was Elisabeth and she was 26 years old.

The lady was making her way home at a leisurely pace and enjoying the pleasant warmth of a late summer evening. The whole situation seemed quite uneventful and I began to wonder why I was being shown all this.

At that moment I was lifted above ground and transported to her house on the outskirts of London. I could see her husband, Timothy, a tall redheaded man, working on some papers in his study. Then the picture changed again, and I saw two burglars, unaware of his presence, breaking into the house from the back.

Alarmed by the noise, Timothy stepped out of the study. On seeing the intruders, he inquired as to the purpose of their visit and, receiving no answer, ordered them out. He tried to push them towards the door, but there was a scuffle. One of the burglars stabbed Timothy twice in the stomach and rushed out of the house. Timothy was discovered by his wife, an hour later, lying lifeless on the floor.

For Elisabeth this tragedy was too much to bear. She never recovered from it.

Timothy had been a sea merchant, trading goods between Britain and the colonies. As the couple did not have children, he devoted himself to his beloved spouse, who basked in the comfort of his care and protection. His demise forced Elisabeth to face life on her own and that was something she never really came to terms with. She sold the house and rented a flat outside London. She spent the rest of her life, up until her passing in 1805, in solitude, mourning her husband, often overcome by sadness and uncertainty.

The last words of Bob's instructions faded in the headphones and I was back in the room.

"How was it?" Michael asked, making no attempt to hide his eagerness.

"Interesting," I replied, not really sure what to make of it all. I described what I had seen. At first, he seemed somewhat surprised but by the end of the story it was all beginning to make sense to him. "Well," he remarked, "taking independent decisions in my life has never been my strong point. But I'm learning. Recently I decided to change jobs, as I haven't been spending enough time with my family. My little daughter was growing up without seeing me around very much and I had to do something about it."

Living out my Dreams

In Focus 25 we were supposed to venture into the territory of religious beliefs, the manifestation of collective perceptions of the afterlife, be it a form of paradise or less agreeable environs.

For me, Focus 25 turned out to be a happy place. That's where dreams come true. Whatever it is you have been longing for, you live it out here.

I struggled through F23 and F24 and found my way into F25 after discovering a small opening in the seemingly infinite dark wall of haphazard thought-forms of a twilight mind.

Eventually I saw a vast blue ocean and I jumped into it without a moment's hesitation. To my right I spotted a huge whale and I merged with its consciousness and its flesh.

It was a long and liberating swim.

I enjoyed the massive powerful movements of the sea-giant, moving up and then going in deep, endlessly, profoundly, without fear of suffocation, because there could be no suffocation there, no limitation and no danger.

Whales, as I found out, are inclined to daydream. The ocean is spacious, so they are not particularly worried about bumping into the shore and plankton consumption does not require any extraordinary levels of mental concentration; so they just swim, going in deep and then resurfacing. The motion of their colossal body creates a hypnotizing rhythm, lasting for thousands of miles and thousands of days and the blessed giants sing their silent song of joy absorbed in the bliss of power and freedom.

I finally left the whale and travelled with dolphins, abandoning myself to their breathtaking fluidity of motion, drunk with the exhilaration of speed and agility. I did not want it to end, and it didn't until I was called back –by Bob's voice – to our so-called Reality that suddenly appeared to be a pale and twisted version of where I had just been.

Visiting the Center of the Earth

The exercise "A Trip to the Center of the Earth" was a wonder. First of all, we were supposed to examine the four elements of our planet.

This time around, Earth, Water and Fire did not trigger very much in the way of images. The Air element, however, was researched at length.

I was flying along with a large flock of white storks, alternating flapping my long wings with moments of breathtaking soaring when I would catch a warm current of air and be borne upwards only to slide down again on meeting a cooler flow till it was time to flap my way back to another ascending stream.

At one point, we were passing over a turquoise river winding endlessly amidst mountains covered in wild forests. I noticed a large black bear standing on a rock and growling angrily at us with all its might. If that had happened down on the ground, it would have been terrifying, but from my location – flying high in the sky – it was just another interesting thing to look at: the river flowing, the clouds floating, the bear roaring... bring it on! What a change in perspective! Everything is very different when seen through the eyes of a bird.

Now the time had come to fly to the center of the Earth. "No problem," I said to myself. "Let's do it!"

I went down closer to the surface and saw an opening in the rocks. I did not hesitate and flew into the gap. I started spiraling down along a seemingly endless tunnel. Bob's voice prompted me to look for a diamond-shaped crystal in the very center of the Earth. The next moment, I was inside the crystal, examining its porous structure. The voice in the headphones suggested looking for intelligences controlling the Earth's maintenance.

I looked around and saw a being. " The lady of the crystal rock" came to my mind. She was a presence in the middle of the crystal, gazing steadily at me. "What is the secret of the Earth?" I asked her in my mind. "Calm and order," she replied quietly with her thoughts.

I stayed motionless for a while enchanted by the play of soft multi-colored light expanding and contracting through the translucent crystal until I heard the countdown bringing me back to our human reality.

The last morning

At the last breakfast, my group was quiet and pensive. We had all crossed into the dimension of death and were no longer quite the same people on coming back. One becomes less judgmental, less inclined to leap to conclusions. I had witnessed trauma and suffering, shock and disorientation among the newly departed souls. I also saw them relieved and happy after moving up and meeting loved ones. There is no death, only a succession of lives – in other worlds with other laws.

If the yoga of the cells does not grant me an eternal life and I pass over one day, I know what I will do. I will head straight to the Welcome Centre in the magnificent peaceful park where I once saw a beautiful sailboat disappearing into heavenly skies.

ISBN 978-2-9700905-0-2
Swiss ISBN Agency
isbn@sbvv.ch